T3-BOA-411

PAINTERS OF TODAY John Bratby

21 *shillings*

PAINTERS OF TODAY

John Bratby A.R.A.

WITH 20 COLOUR PLATES AND AN INTRODUCTION
BY ALAN CLUTTON-BROCK

LONDON : STUDIO BOOKS

Acknowledgments

The author and publishers would like to thank the British Broadcasting Corporation for permission to quote from 'A Conversation with John Bratby' which was broadcast over the Third Programme on the 14th December 1960; and all the collectors and galleries for permission to reproduce their paintings in this volume.

Printed in England by Hunt Barnard and Co. Ltd., The Sign of the Dolphin, Aylesbury Bucks.

John Bratby has lately had a revolving studio built in his garden at Blackheath on the lines of a summer house which can be turned in any direction to catch the sun or avoid the wind. The object of this structure is to enable him to paint any quarter of the surrounding landscape at any season of the year. It is not a landscape that would have interested Salvator Rosa or Turner. In the foreground there is his own garden and house, which is a commodious building of late Victorian character. It is a house for a professional or fairly prosperous business man; it stands in a street of similar dwellings in a most respectable residential neighbourhood, has no claim to architectural interest, and is in no way picturesque. The garden is a fairly large strip at the back, mainly filled with uncut grass but with a swimming pool at one side which looks rather desolate when empty and displaying large areas of raw concrete. This unkempt stretch of ground is in striking contrast to the neat garden on to which it backs, with the close-mown lawns, weedless flower beds and many flowering trees which life in such a neighbourhood, for those who value its standing and amenities, insistently demands. In the middle distance—there is no distance—of the landscape, in the centre of which Bratby in his studio is to be the continually revolving hub, there are more houses like his own and trees rising from a number of well-cultivated plots.

The revolving studio in the garden of his house is not the only one he has; in all he will have four, and he regards a new studio as about the best way of getting rid of surplus income. One large studio on the ground floor contains, amongst much else, a full-sized billiards table on which he and his friends play an advanced kind of snooker requiring two more balls than the usual game. Unlike the grass outside, the green of the cloth gleams bright and spotless, and highlights shine from the polished woodwork. It is a recent acquisition and a most expensive one in which its owner takes great pride, and its presence in the studio explains why snooker players have begun to appear in Bratby's paintings. The rest of the studio consists of the usual workroom, stacked with canvases but containing one or two pieces of the antique furniture which he has lately begun to collect. Much of this is heavily carved Victorian work, but there is also a seventeenth-century Italian cabinet, the doors of which have unfortunately been attacked by worm so that they needed somewhat drastic treatment, namely a coat of thickish yellow paint. On the walls are painted many comminatory inscriptions directed against those who teach or write about art—'those who can't, teach; those who can, do' and the like—an occasional source of embarrassment to the artist, as he admits, when visited by an art critic. Nevertheless, Bratby has himself spent a year, from 1957 to 1958, teaching at the Royal College of Art.

All this tells one a good deal about Bratby himself and his art. In terms of making a living, Bratby is one of the most successful English artists of his particular generation, and this without the loss of prestige incurred by those who take to conciliatory portraiture, painting horses, producing slightly indecent watercolours for English drawing rooms, and other well-tried ways of making art pay. Bratby wanted and intended this success; it did not come to him unexpectedly as it usually does to artists who are not prepared to make any compromise between their own artistic inclinations and those of the public. On the last day of Bratby's final term at the Royal College of Art, Rodrigo Moynihan, Professor of Painting at the time, was going through his papers and tidying things up, anxious to leave, when there was a knock at the door. It was Bratby asking for a word with his teacher, to which Moynihan rather impatiently agreed. The young artist wanted, he said, to be told how to make money out of painting, real money such as would get him a good house, good furniture, good carpets, a motor car. Why he should have gone to Moynihan in search of such valuable information is not to be explained; if Moynihan had known the answer to Bratby's question he would presumably not have been Professor of Painting.

In December 1960 Bratby expressed in a broadcast the satisfaction it has given him to achieve the aim he once put before Moynihan and to be able at last to surround himself with material possessions. He described his 'large late Victorian house' and said that he found it beautiful. With its large garden, he said, it assured him of privacy: 'I think I am a Victorian in this respect and I require sanctuary enormously.' 'Last April,' he continued, 'I got a lot of pleasure from collecting heavily carved wooden furniture, antique Victorian stuff . . . I've got a sideboard for instance which is heavily carved, with three mirrors at the back of it.' The motor car was at that time yet to come, but 'one of these days,' Bratby said, 'I suppose I'll buy a large, tinny, high-powered American car.'

The revolving studio in the garden and the full-sized billiards table appearing first in the studio and soon afterwards in his pictures, imply, what is indeed true, that Bratby is impelled to paint his own immediate surroundings, indoors and out, and hardly anything else. This is quite a natural consequence of the artistic movement with which he has grown up, the movement known as social realism, though not all his contemporaries who adhered to this movement have kept so strictly within their own backyards and back-kitchens.

Social realism began as 'socialist realism', and in the appropriate place, in Russia. There it meant pictures designed to illustrate such matters as the heroism of revolutionaries, the achievements of Russian industrialism, or the dignity of labour. But the first pictures of that kind reveal a considerable acquaintance with contemporary styles in Western painting, and much of what was afterwards condemned as formalism, a reflection of the contradictions of capitalist society. There was, after all, no reason why distortion and elaborate stylization should not be applied to paintings which tell a tale.

Within five years there was a complete and radical transformation and this time not merely of subject but also of style. The Soviet painters, by an extraordinary *tour-de-force*, taught themselves in this brief interval to paint in a manner which is hardly distinguishable from that of Victorian academicians, though one or two bold spirits did contrive to paint in a fashion that would have made them formidable rivals to Sargent. Anything less like social realism, as it was practised in England and France after the second world war, it would be difficult to imagine.

News of these developments in Soviet Russia penetrated slowly to England and France; in this country it was not until the exhibition of Russian paintings, held in Burlington House in 1959, that it was generally recognised how completely the average Soviet artist of the present day resembled his grandfather. In France, Soviet painting was for a long time so little known that it could have done nothing either to promote or to discourage the adoption of the principles on which it was based. All that was understood was that the Soviet approved of painting with a political moral or implication, and this did induce some French artists who were communists to paint, without in the least changing their style, pictures such as Picasso's *Guernica* or Pignon's extremely formalist interpretations of themes like the death of a worker which taught some political lesson.

Paradoxically enough the true originator of social realism in France, and afterwards in England, was an artist whose work seldom has any political moral at all, Francis Gruber, who died in 1948 at the age of thirty-six. An artist of great originality, he was at first influenced by surrealism: it has been pointed out that surrealism often involved a return to realism, though this might well be of the *trompe l'oeil* variety, and Gruber, when he left fantasy behind, began to paint, with a considerable degree of realism, gaunt and emaciated figures with a bleak studio or some other equally depressing interior as background. Later his thin and angular figures reappeared in many French paintings of the social-realist persuasion and their dreary settings seem to have encouraged many younger French and English artists to take an equally poor view of their surroundings.

Many of the French social realists were actually communists, but in England, few if any of the artists who painted in the social-realist manner were more than vaguely to the left. Bratby certainly was not, nor was his choice of subject and style in any way motivated by political opinions. Even when he painted a number of pictures of men suffering from radiation it seems that he had no idea he was doing anything to help ban the bomb; it was just one of those perverse ideas for a subject that artists often get, and Bratby more than most. 'I'm not a social realist painter,' Bratby said in his broadcast, but of course he is in the sense that he paints like one; Duccio might just as well have protested that he was not a primitive. If one asks Bratby why he should have decided to take up such a method of painting all that he can say, and all that anyone can say, is that it was in the air and that he, Jack Smith, Edward Middleditch, Derrick Greaves, and some others took it up just as a few years later many art students inevitably took to action painting. The English artists may, in fact, be said to be more realist than social, and not always so very realist either, since the vein of expressionism was even stronger in them than in their French contemporaries.

Bratby was born in 1928, the son of a wine-taster who afterwards worked as a clerk in the offices of Gordons, the makers of gin. At school art was the only subject in which he took any interest or showed any aptitude. He went into the army as a conscript, but after nine weeks it was discovered that he was extremely short-sighted and he was invalided out with an ex-service grant which enabled him to study at

Kingston Art School. There he worked for the Intermediate Examination in Arts and Crafts and failed.

The grant was withdrawn and Bratby went off on his own and painted for a year, supporting himself by working in a toy factory, a brewery and on a wharf. His paintings were of sunflowers, his room, the breakfast table, in fact everything that surrounded him. He also painted murals on the walls of his room. He tried again to pass the Intermediate Examination, failed again, and went on working for another year by himself in his lodgings. Then he decided to apply for admission to the Slade School, and submitted a sheaf of his drawings. Both Sir William Coldstream and Claude Rogers were impressed by his ability, but their enthusiasm was checked when Bratby was shown into the room where they had spent a long day interviewing students wishing to join the school. He told them that he had made further inquiries since sending in his application and had been informed that the Royal College of Art was a better school than the Slade. Between the Slade and the College, sometimes described at the Slade as the government school, there exists much the same friendly rivalry as between Eton and Harrow. At the Slade, with its tradition of high seriousness and with some of the most conscientious of the painters of the Euston Road Group on its staff, there is a feeling that the art produced at the College is perhaps a little showy. It was therefore disconcerting for Coldstream to be asked by a raw student whether he could help him to get into the Royal College. But he picked up the telephone, got through to Robin Darwin, the principal of the Royal College, and said that he had with him a student whose drawings he thought the College ought to see. Bratby was duly admitted to the Royal College.

At the Royal College he observed that there were a number of unoccupied rooms under the roof of the vast and rambling Victorian building. Like the people who once lived with their families and even their cattle on some upper floor of the Tzar's palace without anyone suspecting their presence, Bratby moved himself into one of these rooms with a camp bed and a paraffin stove. He had very little money and by living in the College he was saved rent and the cost of travelling from the suburbs every day. His room jutted out and ran along the top storey of the Victoria and Albert Museum and connoisseurs of things like *netsukes* or knife handles visiting the museum were often assailed by a strong and inexplicable smell of frying kippers.

Bratby made his mark on the school in other ways. True to the principles of social realism in England he collected dustbins from all over the school, brought them to his rooms and painted whole groups of them. Once he took a fancy to a skeleton that had been provided for the instruction of anatomy; he was not interested in anatomy but was fascinated by the shape of the bones. Later when living in the house of his parents-in-law he caused similar inconvenience by his habit of removing the groceries from the kitchen and taking them to his studio in order to paint them.

His habit of painting very thick began while he was at the College and he thinks it was the result of the wild excitement he felt at being there. The use of thick paint is, he thinks, 'the natural result of vigour and energy in a painting'. He applied for and was granted an extra allowance of artist's materials.

He was awarded a Royal College of Art travelling scholarship and an Abbey Minor scholarship, one of those prizes which in the past were supposed to take British artists to Rome so that they might study Michelangelo and Raphael and thereafter found a great school of mural painting in this country. Bratby went to Italy but the visit was not a success. He did not like the taste of garlic and the foreign cooking upset his stomach. In his first novel, *Breakdown*, published in 1960 and to be referred to later, he wrote a poignant description, obviously based on bitter experience, of a young English painter in Rome who was suffering from jaundice contracted because 'the food was unhygienically sold in Italy'; this painter then bought three packets of Quaker Oats in a grocer's shop where 'the sight of this good English food made his eyes shine'. Moreover Bratby could not speak a word of Italian, and he does not seem to have been much interested in the paintings he saw. Nor since then has he taken much interest in old masters or paid many visits to the National Gallery; he even feels that it might be unwise to do so, that it might put him off his stroke. When it is pointed out that so strikingly original and idiosyncratic an artist as Cézanne continually visited the Louvre, Bratby's answer is that Cézanne, however great an artist he may have been, was never altogether sure of himself and suffered from doubts.

Bratby on the other hand has complete self-confidence; he knows for certain that he can do what he sets out to do though it may be, as he concedes, a small thing, or possibly, as he also concedes, not a small thing. Asked during his broadcast whether he had ever received criticism of his pictures which he considered just, he replied that he had received quite a lot of flattering criticism. Asked, rather pressingly, whether he had ever received any unflattering criticism which he considered just, he replied, rather surprisingly, that he had. But this, he added, was from critics who were looking at his pictures through a brick wall. If he tried to put himself in their shoes he could manage to see his paintings as 'mountains and valleys of insensitively applied paint'. 'So I do consider their criticisms just—it's just that they're looking at them through the wrong spectacles, that's all.'

After his experience in Italy Bratby is quite sure that it would not be of any use to him to travel abroad, even though this could be put down as expenses and so help with the income tax, which troubles him a good deal nowadays. It might be thought that even though he might not want to visit foreign picture galleries he might still find subjects abroad, but he has tried it, and, as one might expect, it will not do; away from his own immediate surroundings his painting, he thinks, is apt to get sentimental. But though he has no wish to look at pictures abroad he has begun to buy some handsome art books, including a volume of reproductions after Kokoschka, an artist with whom he seems to be in sympathy, and he is evidently not afraid that studying these reproductions will do him any harm.

After leaving the Royal College he worked with great intensity for some months. It was then, he feels, that he found himself and worked out the kind of painting he most wanted to do. And so he prepared for his first one-man show. On the face of it no young artist could have been further from success than Bratby at this moment. He was in the habit of painting very large pictures, which dealers always mistrust; their customers, they believe, all live in small rooms and have space only for small cabinet pictures. His subjects were the reverse of attractive, and he would or could do nothing to make them so; in his own opinion, he paints better when, as he puts it, he is painting 'in opposition', presumably in opposition to the taste of his customers. For this reason he once painted and showed two huge pictures, six or seven feet high, of empty waterclosets, though it is true that he was also interested in the shape of the bowl, pipes and cisterns. His thickly piled, slashed-on paint was very harsh in its effect, the colour was unconciliatory, and the faces of his figures were for the most part desperately and deliberately ugly. Apart from the distortion of the features such as usually results from the use of an expressionistic technique, Bratby could always be relied on to add thirty years to the prettiest young woman.

But the art-loving and art-buying public has been conditioned to take almost anything from any artist of talent, and after Picasso they are certainly not to be frightened by an ugly face. When Bratby held his first exhibition in 1954 at the Beaux-Arts Gallery, where Mrs Lessore has done so much to discover and bring to light the talent of young and previously unknown artists, this was an unqualified success; his work attracted much attention from the critics and he sold more than £500 worth of pictures, a large amount for a painter who had not exhibited before. Since then he has never, as they say, looked back.

After this we have been constantly able to observe life with the Bratbys, almost the only subject that he cares to paint. It has continued year after year, like a serial story which is all middle and no beginning or end, or like catching glimpses of what the next-door neighbours, at once familiar and enigmatic, are doing over the garden wall. Not the slightest attempt is made to arrange things for our inspection; nothing is put away tidily but everything and everybody is always all over the place. This, one is made to feel, is how Bratby likes it, perhaps in reality and certainly in his pictures. Although these are artists living here this hardly seems to be the disorder of Bohemia, the litter of the studio; whether by accident or design it is more like the casual comfort of the working man's living room, where a cosy warmth is all that matters, where there are no appearances to keep up, and no organised social life is expected to occur within doors, a private world from which nosey parkers are firmly excluded. By sheer strength of character, or perhaps as a result of the artist's usual indifference to conventional standards, Bratby has imposed his own background on the trim avenues of Blackheath.

This impression, that we are peering into a very private world, is no illusion. Bratby himself says that he is 'a pretty hermit-like sort of character', and as he described it he seems to be engaged in a constant struggle to keep people out. 'I have sixty-two bolts and locks in my house, they still get in my studio,' he has complained. A few must be let in if he is to get his snooker, but otherwise there is hardly any social life. He paints all day, keeping regular hours, not enjoying the work—'It's an unpleasant thing for me, the task I've set myself'—but uncomfortable if he has not done enough and feeling satisfaction if he has. Then if there is no snooker, the television, and, one gathers, nothing else.

In his novel Bratby has given an exaggerated but perhaps not wholly impossible description of the sort of subjects he might conceivably paint; he refers to two pictures entitled *Still Water in a Blocked-up Guttering* and *Choked-up Carburetter*. One doubts whether any earlier artist has accepted so whole-heartedly the casual and even repellent circumstances of everyday life as a fit theme for painting. Some of Van Gogh's works, such as the *Café at Arles* or *Van Gogh's Bedroom in Arles* may perhaps be offered as a comparison, but in Van Gogh's bedroom the bed is at least made and everything is reasonably tidy. Would Bratby, one wonders, care to paint a bed unless it happened to have been left unmade? He himself feels there is some affinity between his art and that of Stanley Spencer, and in spite of the very great difference in the technique of the two artists, in spite of Bratby's rough handling and Spencer's neat treatment of detail, some of Spencer's paintings do have rather the same quality as Bratby's, the same ready acceptance of all the tritest details of modern life. Spencer certainly welcomes capricious disorder, and it is a conspicuous feature of some of his religious paintings. Though Courbet claimed to be such a realist, sumptuous baskets of fruit had to be sent to him during his imprisonment in order that he might have subjects to paint. But Spencer, one feels, and Bratby also, would have been content to go on painting the cell itself with relish and conviction; whatever furniture the government provided for its captive would have been enough.

One modification of the object before his eyes that both Spencer and Bratby allow themselves is enlargement. Spencer's portraits for example—the most grimly realistic of his works—were apt to be larger than life, and Bratby will often blow things up to twice their natural size. If realism is to be taken literally, which it never is, enlargement to more than life-size is of course unrealistic, but then so is the universal practice of painting things smaller than they are and on the face of it both changes of scale would seem to be equally justifiable. In practice, enlargement does seem to be rather odder and more startling than diminution of size. In the past it has been done often enough by the Egyptians, the Greeks, the Byzantines and the Italians of the High Renaissance. But this was usually when sculpture had to be applied or related to a large building, or when mural painting was used to decorate a large room. Enlargement in easel pictures was less common and is largely a modern device. It is apt to surprise, to make the objects represented on such a scale seem more shocking than if they were merely life-size, and we may be sure that this particular effect of enlargement was not unwelcome to Bratby. It need not always be so; in Middleditch's later paintings, for example, enlargement has the effect of detaching what he paints from reality and making it appear more romantic, but at least there can be no doubt that in Bratby's paintings making things larger than life intensifies the harsh appearance of the machine-made modern world.

Enlargement is also an appropriate device for painters of expressionist tendency; if particular colours and shapes are to be given particular emotional overtones, as is the object of the expressionist artist and as Van Gogh explicitly intended, an increase in size, such as does in fact occur in some of Van Gogh's paintings as well as in a number of later expressionist works, adds emphasis and force, underlining, as it were, the character of the shapes and reinforcing the impact of the colour. Enlargement has much the same effect in Bratby's pictures and may well be a symptom of his expressionist leanings. He used once to get indignant with critics who said that his painting was expressionist, but now he is inclined to think that they may have been right. In his novel he comments on his own paintings through the mouth of one of his own characters. 'Bratby,' a young art student is made to say, 'is a marvellous painter; he has painted anything from your dustbin to your kitchen sink, and with the passion of Soutine and the drawing of Kokoschka.' This certainly sounds like expressionism.

It may be thought necessary to ask whether there is any really good reason for painting such things as dustbins or cartons from the grocer's shop. The fact that their appearance in a picture may startle and annoy is really not a sufficient reason, nor is there here, as in many French social-realist paintings, a political motive to justify the choice of an unattractive subject, while even if there were such a motive we should very soon get tired of having it rubbed in all the time. One reason, and quite a good one, is that the artist confronted with something irretrievably banal is put on his mettle to make it seem exciting when he has painted it. To convert objects which are conspicuously lifeless, such as the arid products of a modern mechanical process, into forms which are charged with nervous energy, is a feat which Bratby frequently attempts; his large and lumpish billiards table with its hard French-polished surface positively challenges him to make its component parts bristle with vitality.

But, of course, by no means everything Bratby paints is as aggressively unpicturesque as a dustbin or a watercloset. Most of the things that appear in his pictures have not been put there in defiance of the taste of the public, but simply because they belong to his everyday life, and there is often an excellent motive, one that has its roots deep in the artist's character, for painting what is familiar. There seems to be a natural division, persistently recurring in artists of almost every school of painting, between those who prefer to paint what is strange or wonderful, and those who prefer to paint what is ordinary. Even among the Italian painters of the Renaissance, who almost always had their subjects set for them, there is a world of difference between such backgrounds as those of Signorelli, with their unearthly pinnacles of rock, and the domestic interiors or placid landscapes, against which many other artists of the time chose to set their figures. Or again, Turner would have preferred the Alps to the village allotments, but Pissarro's choice would have been the other way about.

Bratby is emphatically on the side of the ordinary, too emphatically sometimes, but at other times quite naturally so. It is part of his character that he cannot be otherwise, any more than Jan Steen could be expected to paint the subjects that appealed to Veronese. It is true that an artist of the present day who has such a preference is likely to confront the spectator with objects that seem far more banal and ugly than anything to be found in paintings of the past, but that is because objects of everyday use are inevitably, as a result of industrial development, more distressing to the eye than they used to be. There are dream kitchens, no doubt, and stainless steel sinks to the appearance of which some industrial designer has given a lot of thought, but these hardly belong to the kind of world the Bratbys have made for themselves and, in general, the gas stove is likely to be a more disconcerting object, when it appears in a picture, than the open hearth of a seventeenth-century Dutch kitchen.

There seems to be very little connection between the choice of everyday things for subjects and the style in which they are painted. The scene may be represented in minute detail, as in many Dutch paintings of the seventeenth century, or with the grace of handling and the delicious quality of paint that Chardin achieved. In modern times the treatment might be impressionist or, by contrast, expressionist. In the work of Stanley Spencer there is a return to the minute description of the Dutch, but it is worth observing that in his larger and more important works he did not so much paint the commonplace things of today as of his youth. Possessed of an astonishing visual memory he could draw out of his mind, inspired by nostalgia for the past, such things as a Japanese lantern or a housemaid's cap as he had seen them forty years before. In general no social realist in France or England has used anything but a broad treatment, though the Russians, of course, have been compelled to describe every detail. It is only the imaginative artists of the West, the surrealists and Spencer himself, whose principal works are all mythological and who regarded his straightforward landscapes and paintings of flowers as potboilers, who have dared to return to the detailed realism of the past.

Bratby's technique and style is essentially expressionist, and it is obvious that Van Gogh has been a major influence on his work, as on that of many earlier expressionists. His is an impulsive way of painting, or at least the success of his method depends on giving the impression that it is impulsive. Every brush-stroke has to appear impetuous and alive, and if any passage should seem slack it has to be re-worked with a new access of energy. At the same time he does not, as he himself says, rush at his work in an emotional frenzy. The placing of his figures sometimes appears haphazard and arbitrary, so that a head and two arms may appear right in the foreground with scarcely any indication of a body attached to it, the rest of the figure being cut off by the bottom edge of the canvas. This seems as strange as the detached limbs which occasionally appear protruding inwards from the edge of the picture in Cézanne's early figure paintings, and there cannot be much doubt that here such an awkward arrangement has only come about because at this early stage of his career Cézanne worked without much forethought, without any planning of the mechanical part of the composition. But Bratby claims that he does in fact give a good deal of thought to the placing of the figures, and at least it can be said that there is a reason, other than a mere wish to fill up the canvas, for some of his strangest arrangements of figures. Sometimes, for example, the fragments of a figure at the edge of the canvas are those fragments of himself that he could see. 'I had,' he said, 'to paint my own activity of painting the picture, and so the painting of the girl many times also included me painting the picture. And all the attendant paraphernalia of paint tubes and palette and so on, and brushes making the marks, and so on and so forth.' Asked, during his broadcast, if he thought it was his honesty that made him want to paint absolutely everything that he could see, including these fragments of himself, he said, yes, he supposed it could be called honesty.

To many expressionist artists colour is of particular importance as a means of provoking an emotional response; for this purpose it may be of more importance than form. Van Gogh certainly claimed that the actual shapes in his painting of his bedroom at Arles gave an impression of repose, but he seems to have had a much more passionate response to the colour of his sunflowers, as appears not only from his letters but also from the pictures themselves. Bratby's colour is seldom as vivid as that of Van Gogh's later pictures, or as that of the early expressionists who took their palette from the *fauves*, and here he is in line with most of the social realists of his time who avoid bright or cheerful colour quite deliberately as being unsuited to any representation of the drab world they portray. But even when sombre, Bratby's colour can be strong. It is invented rather than observed, not based on any close study of values, but well adapted to the character of the scene. At times it shows considerable originality, as in the very positive effect produced by his ingenious use of whites. But he is certainly not an artist whose colour one instinctively thinks of first; for him colour is often an auxiliary rather than a primary means of expression.

So it is the forms that have to do most of the work. Everything in his pictures comes out as it is written, in the artist's own handwriting, not at all an elegant hand, but one whose individual character is immediately recognisable. Because of the opportunity they give him to display and reiterate linear rhythms, he welcomes repeated patterns in his painting: the divisions between the blocks of a parquet floor, the circles and intersecting lines on a lace curtain, the constant repetition of the same shapes in row upon row of bottles and pans on the kitchen shelf. At first sight the arum lilies that appear in several of his recent portraits might be thought part of a flowery pattern of a fabric rather than flowers existing in three dimensions, and even the lines on a face must make a pattern and for that reason are more pronounced than the contours.

But at the same time every object is made to retain its individual character; in the huddle of objects in his kitchen scenes it is always possible to identify the various objects, to distinguish, for example, a milk bottle from any other kind of bottle. His faces certainly do not lose any of their character because at first sight he seems to have used them merely as a pretext for constructing a pattern of angular lines. It would be impossible to reconcile two such conflicting aims without a very sharp eye for the individual and distinguishing features of objects, something like the botanist's eye which can at once discover an unusual species in the hedgerow. This may help to explain why Bratby is so determined to paint only his own immediate surroundings; an expert on the flora of the British Isles could not be expected to use his acumen if set down suddenly in an exotic landscape.

Social realism is now the latest movement in art but one, the latest being action painting and the various forms of abstract expressionism that have developed out of it. To be overtaken by another and completely different fashion while still young is not an altogether agreeable experience, and the references to action painting in Bratby's novel are acid enough. Some of the small group of painters who, along with Bratby, developed the British variety, neither particularly social nor particularly realist, of social realism, have evidently grown discontented with their former way of painting and some have departed very far from it. They have had before them the inspiring example of their own Professor of Painting at the Royal College of Art. Recently Rodrigo Moynihan, who for a considerable time had been practising the kind of realism developed by the Euston Road School and had some success as a portrait painter, startled everyone by suddenly becoming an out and out action painter and in consequence resigning from the Royal Academy. So Middleditch has become a romantic and Derrick Greaves has come near to abstraction.

The new movement has had no such effect on Bratby, but for all that there has been some change. He has recently been painting a number of portraits, mostly of young women, and he himself says, as many portrait painters have said before him, that he wants to paint the souls of these girls. This cannot, of course, mean more than that the painted face should tell one a good deal about the character of the sitter, and it is not always clear whether the artist merely wishes it to give as much information as the real face, or whether he hopes it will reveal more. If more, then there is the obvious risk that the artist will allow his own feelings about his sitters to colour and distort their image and will, in fact, put more of himself than of his sitter into the portrait.

But whatever the artist may mean by painting the soul and however unlikely it is that he will succeed in doing so, it is an aim which no really orthodox social realist would be likely to put before himself. In the strictly social-realist picture, such as many of the French and more of the Russians have painted, human beings are hardly conceived as individuals. The figures that appear in them are more likely to be representatives of some class, submerged proletarians in a capitalist civilisation, sturdy peasants, heroic defenders of the revolution, or, as in Guttuso's well-known painting of dancers, degenerate admirers of abstract art. Even the English social realists, though much less inclined to a classification of types, have usually been more concerned to make the figures fit the background than to make the background fit the figures; they have looked for the right sort of person to go with the dustbin. So Bratby's new interest in the character of the individual may be considered a significant deviation.

At first sight it might be thought that the subjects of Bratby's portraits have come out as typical Bratby figures, such as appeared in many of his earlier interiors, worried and preoccupied people, haggard from the cares of housekeeping, or perhaps from some deeper cause of anxiety. Yet inevitably, since these are portraits, the face has become the focus of the picture to an extent that the faces of the figures in his earlier paintings seldom were. Moreover in some of the recent interiors with groups of figures, such as the series of paintings of snooker players round the billiards table, the features are more sharply differentiated than they used to be and the spectator is made aware of the psychological situation which the artist has chosen to represent. A figure in the foreground, for instance, may be frowning with impatience at the extreme deliberation with which his opponent is making his stroke, and we are given quite a clear idea of the different characters of the two men. In effect, human beings are now beginning to emerge, not exactly in triumph, but still with their individuality preserved, from the great clutter of still-life and the gross assembly of mass-produced objects among which they were sunk in the past.

This emergence of a more humanist approach to painting coincided with Bratby's first venture as a novelist and may well have been encouraged by his practice of this other art. His book, *Breakdown,* met with a curious reception; many critics were evidently appalled by the numerous scenes of unmitigated squalor described in it, but it sold well enough, perhaps because it had been so vigorously attacked, and it was recommended by the Book Society. The main character in the novel is James Brady, a painter, who might be John Bratby were it not for the fact that we are explicitly told he is nothing of the sort—if it were so, Bratby explains to his readers, 'I would indeed be an Awful Mess'—and if John Bratby were not actually discussed as a separate person by some of the characters in the novel. Thus Brady himself says that Bratby is a better draughtsman than he, but that he, Brady, has more humanity in his work; Bratby does not sell as well as Brady, but Bratby will 'probably get a knighthood if he doesn't blot his copybook'. As far as the art of the real and the imaginary painter is concerned, these differences do not seem to be important; Bratby and Brady, we are told, 'are both of the same generation, moulded in the same moulds, taught by the same generation of painters, and both expressing the tensions and unrest of our atom-bomb-threatened age'.

The essential difference between the two is that Brady goes to the bad, though it is not quite clear whether Brady is Bratby but for the grace of God. Brady's breakdown is a direct result of a series of unattractive love affairs with women who all seem to be half mad and much less agreeable than his own wife; the first of them blackmails Brady into keeping up with her by threatening to reveal the affair to his wife. It is, we are left in no doubt, a moral breakdown and no mere misfortune; these love affairs set Brady wandering all over the country and prevent him from any attempt to continue painting, except when he returns home and tries to reform himself. Wife and home, we are told, would have cured Brady and it is only at home that he can work. As soon as he lets go of Mrs Brady's hand, 'Brady's appearance begins to change into that of a gorilla'. The conclusion, a demonstration that the wages of sin is death, is not very logical; Brady is eventually killed by accident and as a result of a fairly innocuous decision to make a collection of swords. But it is not easy to know just how to kill off the undeserving.

Whatever else it may be this is a highly moral book and one which teaches a lesson that might have won the approval of Samuel Smiles. The reader is constantly reminded that Brady, who really got very little enjoyment out of becoming a gorilla, could have avoided his awful fate if only he had stayed at home, risen early, worked long and regular hours and avoided the company of lunatic girls. He had, in fact, only to follow the pattern of Bratby's own life. The whole story is the exact opposite of the theme of the novel *The Moon and Sixpence* which Somerset Maugham based more or less on the life of Gauguin; in order to paint great pictures Maugham's hero had to leave his wife and live just such a wandering life of poverty and squalor as Brady did. The artist hero of Joyce Cary's novel *The Horse's Mouth*, whose pictures Bratby was commissioned to paint when the book was made into a film, leads a life even more precisely like that which Bratby held up to reprobation in his own novel and, indeed, one may even wonder whether it was his association with this story which induced him to write what amounts to a direct contradiction of Joyce Cary's idea of an appropriate life for the artist to live.

Maugham's is very much the romantic view, and perhaps for that reason to be viewed with mistrust. Moreover he was no doubt induced to take this view by the fact that his idea of a happy ending, one that he has contrived in a surprisingly large number of his plays and stories, involves the escape of some man from some woman; again and again he has followed the pattern of the 'Divorce Novelette' which Samuel Butler once sketched and has shown that, as Butler put it, 'faint heart never yet got rid of fair lady'. But after making due allowance for this singular prejudice, Maugham's view of the artist as a natural outcast and enemy of the ordered way of life may still be thought to have some measure of truth in it. Those who take this view may point to the fact that Bratby's devotion to duty has recently been rewarded by his election as an associate of the Royal Academy. But this is not really as significant as might be thought, or as it would have been in the past. None of Bratby's contemporaries has entertained that distrust of the Academy which has made so many older artists refuse to exhibit there and decline to join it. It may be that they are more cynical than their elders, or conceivably they are more simple, but in any case they are more willing to accept any good that may be got out of the place.

One answer to those who doubt whether it can be good for an artist to avoid all adventure, to live like a sound and cautious business man, and to look upon life, as Bratby says he does, as an enlarged game of Monopoly, may be that Bratby does after all put a good deal of unconformity into his art, a rich disorder into those of his works which are manifestly painted in opposition. When an artist refused the Legion of Honour, what, Degas once asked, was the good of this when his art had obviously accepted it; it may well be that Bratby can safely accept conventional rewards since his art as obviously rejects them.

A more difficult and perhaps impossible question to answer is whether Bratby will continue to be able to find enough material for his art within a few suburban square yards. Many artists have required little more, but they have usually been men like Renoir or Bonnard who invariably found charm or beauty in flowers, in faces, and all everyday things. Artists like Toulouse-Lautrec or Forain, who viewed humanity in much the same spirit as Bratby views his kitchen, have usually needed to go further afield, to the law courts, for example, or the music halls. It is possible that his new study of humanity may in the end bring him out of his seclusion to brave the manifold dangers which, if we believe his novel, must confront the artist with every step that he takes outside his home.

The Plates

1. **Dustbins:** 1954. Oil on hardboard 44 × 40 in.
The Royal College of Art.
2. **Still-life with Chipfryer:** 1954. Oil on hardboard $51\frac{1}{4}$ × $36\frac{3}{4}$ in.
The Trustees of the Tate Gallery.
3. **Carel Weight, Jean and table-top:** 1955. Oil on hardboard 48 × 40 in.
Collection of the Artist.
4. **Jean at Basin:** 1956. Oil on board 48 × $30\frac{3}{4}$ in.
Collection of Mr. Brinsley Ford.
5. **Window, Self-portrait, Jean and hands**: 1957. Oil on hardboard 4 ft. × 12 ft.
The Trustees of the Tate Gallery.
6. **Antonia Packenham:** 1957. Oil on hardboard 6 ft. × 4 ft.
Collection of the Artist.
7. **The Painter painting portraits of a Hornsey art student:** 1958. Oil on hardboard 6 ft. × 12 ft.
Collection of the Artist.
8. **Adam and Eve:** 1958. Oil on canvas 6 ft. × 8 ft.
Collection of Mr. Alexander A. Dubenchick.
9. **Sarah in the Bath, 1:** 1958. Oil on canvas 5 ft. × 3 ft. 6 in.
French & Co. Inc., New York.
10. **David amongst the Sunflowers:** 1959. Oil on canvas 44 × 34 in.
Collection of Mr. Brinsley Ford.
11. **The Artist's Wife:** 1960. Oil on Canvas 32 × 48 in.
Collection of the Artist.
12. **Sleepless Nights:** 1960. Oil on canvas 54 × 15 in.
Collection of Mr. Kenneth Horne.
13. **The Return of Gloria Bishop:** 1960. Oil on canvas 48 × 34 in.
Collection of the Artist.
14. **Chalking the Cue:** 1960. Oil on canvas 32 × 46 in.
Collection of the Artist.
15. **Self-Portrait at the Temperance Billiard Hall:** 1960. Oil on canvas 32 × 46 in.
Collection of the Artist.
16. **He threw a rose at her feet:** 1960. Oil on canvas 72 × 24 in.
Collection of the Artist.
17. **Gloria with eccentric construction:** 1960. Oil on canvas 72 × 24 in.
Collection of Mr. Michael Osterweil.
18. **Gloria, Sunflowers and Hidden Earwigs:** 1960. Oil on canvas 42 × 28 in.
Collection of Mr. E. Murphy.
19. **Gloria with Sunflowers:** 1960. Oil on canvas 44 × 34 in.
Collection of the Artist.
20. **Gloria in revolving Studio:** 1960. Oil on canvas 6 ft. × 2 ft.
Collection of the Artist.

1

2

3

4

6

10

12

13

CIGARETTES
"MEDIUM"

15

16

18

19

20